SOCCER SKILLS

The Diagram Group

BROCKHAMPTON
DIAGRAM
GUIDES

Soccer Skills

First published in Great Britain in 1997 by
Brockhampton Press Ltd
20 Bloomsbury Street
London
WC1 2QA
a member of the Hodder Headline Group PLC

ISBN 1-86019-748-5

Also in this series:
Calligraphy
Card Games
How the Body Works
Identifying Architecture
Kings and Queens of Britain
Magic Tricks
Party Games

Introduction

Soccer Skills describes how to perform the basic skills of soccer. Clear, step-by-step instructions and diagrams show you how to kick the ball and control it with your feet, head and chest. The lessons contained in this compact guide are essential both for those learning to play soccer for the first time, and for players who wish to check and improve their technique. In the first two sections of the book you will learn the basic principles of soccer and essential facts about the field and equipment. The remainder of the book describes the skills you need to practise in order to become a proficient player.

Contents

Basic principles

Football games have been known for a very long time –
for example, a version of football was played in China in
200 BC. Soccer as we know it today evolved in England
in the mid-19th century. The Football Association was
formed in 1863, and the Football League in 1888. The
Fédération Internationale de Football Association (FIFA),
the governing body of international football, was formed
in 1904, and the first World Cup was organized in 1908.
Soccer has been included in the Olympic Games
since 1904.

The object in soccer is to score more goals than the
opposing team. Except at throw-ins, the goalkeeper is the
only player allowed to play the ball with his hands or
arms, and he may do so only within his own penalty area
(see pages 8 and 9). Other players in the team are
penalized for using their hands or arms. The major skill
in soccer is thus to be able to kick the ball and control it
with the feet (**1**). The head (**2**), chest (**3**) and thighs (**4**)
can also be used to control the ball.

Once a player has gained possession of the ball he can use it to his team's advantage by passing it to a team-mate, dribbling with it or shooting it at the goal. His opponents will try to reclaim possession by tackling him, intercepting his pass or stopping his shot. A player may not kick, trip or push an opponent, or tackle in a dangerous manner. Players are penalized for illegal tackles and for any of the other fouls outlined in the rules. For persistent infringements, a player may be cautioned and finally sent off for the duration of the game. A player sent off during the game may not be replaced.

A football team has eleven members (excluding substitutes): a goalkeeper plus ten outfield players who are either defenders, mid-field players or attackers. The goalkeeper's function is to stop the ball by catching it whenever possible, or punching or pushing it to safety behind the goal line. He must learn to 'clear' the ball by kicking or throwing it to a team-mate. The defenders are the goalkeeper's allies. Their main function is to make sure that he is not exposed to the full strength of the opposing attack. Defenders must be able to tackle to regain possession for their team. They must also be able to halt the progress of the opposing team by 'marking' (remaining close to an opponent so that it is difficult for him to become involved in the play).

The mid-field player is an all-purpose player. He should help his defence when they are defending and support his attack when they are bearing down on the opposing goal. He must always be aware of what is going on and needs highly developed passing and intercepting skills.

The attackers must provide goals for their team; they need to have fast reactions, courage and a calm approach to scoring opportunities which can arise and disappear in a matter of seconds. A forward or attacker must be able to head the ball, dribble and outwit defenders. He must seek to create opportunities for his colleagues to score when he is unable to do so himself.

Field and equipment

FIELD OF PLAY

Soccer is played on a rectangular field (the length of the field exceeds its width). It is bounded by touchlines (**a**) and goal lines (**b**), both of which are part of the playing area. The halfway line (**c**) divides the field. No line may be wider than 12.7 cm (5 in). At each corner of the field is a flag on a post (**d**). Centred on each of these flags is a quarter circle with a radius of 91 cm (3 ft). Flags (**e**) on either side of the centre line are optional and must be set back at least 91 cm (3 ft) from the touchline. The centre

FIELD OF PLAY

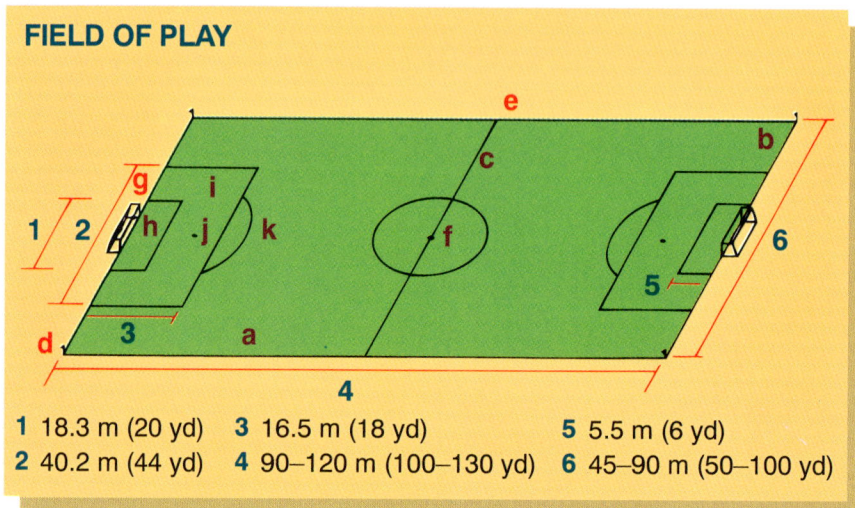

1 18.3 m (20 yd)	**3** 16.5 m (18 yd)	**5** 5.5 m (6 yd)
2 40.2 m (44 yd)	**4** 90–120 m (100–130 yd)	**6** 45–90 m (50–100 yd)

circle (**f**) has a radius of 9.1 m (10 yd). At either end of the field there is a goal (**g**) and a goal area (**h**) enclosed in a larger penalty area (**i**). The posts and crossbar of the goal must be the same width and equal to the width of the goal line. Nets may be attached to the goals and the ground behind. The penalty mark (**j**) is 11.09 m (12 yd) from the goal line. The arc of a circle (**k**), centred on the penalty mark and with a radius of 9.1 m (10 yd), extends outside the penalty area.

BALL

A soccer ball (**l**) is made of leather or another approved material. A full-sized ball must have a circumference of 68.6–71.1 cm (27–28 in). At the start of a game it must weigh 396–453 g (14–16 oz) and should be inflated to a pressure of 600–700 g/cm^2 (9–10½ lb/in^2). The ball may not be changed during a game without the referee's permission.

GOAL

BALL

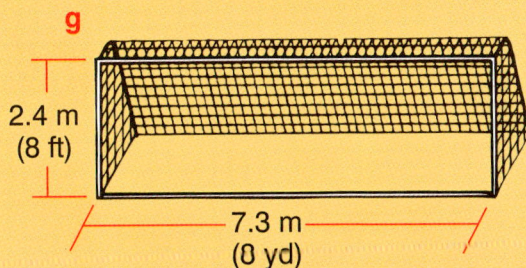

g

2.4 m
(8 ft)

7.3 m
(8 yd)

l

Kicking skills

LOW DRIVE

'Keep the ball on the ground' is a common cry from coaches. Doing so requires practice and a good kicking technique. Learning to drive the ball low allows you to play long or short passes and create the shots goalkeepers like least – fierce drives along the ground.

The part of your foot to use when driving the ball low is the instep. Your weight distribution and balance are important factors as you approach the ball. Keeping your eyes on the ball is vital.

The key to the low drive is to place your non-kicking foot alongside the ball – *not* behind it – and to keep all your weight on that foot as you go to kick the ball. Your body should be completely over the ball.

LOW DRIVE

Take a long stride and swing your kicking leg in a straight line along the path of the approaching ball. If you pull your foot across this line, you will hook the shot; if you make contact to the side of the line, you will slice it.

Drive your foot through, making sure that you strike the ball at its mid-point. Do not get your foot underneath the ball because this will loft it into the air. At the point of contact, the knee of your kicking leg should be over the ball. Leaning back will cause you to loft the ball so keep your weight forward.

Swing your leg through after contact. If you have kicked the ball properly your leg will follow through along the same line the ball has taken.

Practise the low drive with both feet.

LOFTED DRIVE

LOFTED DRIVE

To loft the ball with the instep of your foot, reverse some of the techniques for keeping the ball on the ground.

Take a long stride into the kicking position and swing your foot at the ball. Again make sure that you focus attention on the ball and that you are kicking in a straight line along its path, not across it.

Place your standing foot slightly behind the ball and to one side of it. Lean back a little but not so far as to upset your balance.

Strike the ball at its lower half with the inside of your foot. You should aim to get your foot underneath the ball to loft it into the air.

As with the low drive, follow through is crucial for both power and accuracy.

HALF-VOLLEY

Another controlled style of kicking is the half-volley. This involves playing the ball at the moment it hits the ground so timing is crucial.

The first principle is to judge exactly where the ball is going to land. You will not succeed if you miscalculate so keep your eyes fixed on the ball all the way as it drops.

The half-volley is a flexible technique. You can kick it with any part of your foot. If you lean over the ball as in the low drive you can keep it on the ground. If you lean back as in the lofted drive you can hoist it in the air. In all cases, good control and a deft touch are needed to guide the ball in the direction you want it to go.

If you are shooting for goal or making a long clearance
on the half-volley, make sure your swing follows
through. If you are playing a shorter more controlled
pass, check your swing so the ball does not overshoot.

HALF-VOLLEY

VOLLEY

To intercept the ball when it is in the air you must learn to volley. This is a tricky but very important skill. A lower ball is easier to volley because you can achieve a longer back swing. A high ball is the most difficult because there is no time or room to wind up a massive kick. To volley correctly will take practice but it is worth all the effort.

Because the ball is high you must lean away from it to make a cleaner contact. The higher the bounce, the further back you must lean. If you do not bend away from the ball there will be no room for you to swing your leg.

To keep the shot low, pivot your body so your kicking leg meets the ball on a horizontal plane – like a baseball bat hitting a pitch. Use your arms (as in the picture) to keep your balance.

You can volley the ball with any part of your foot except the toe. Snap your foot at the ball with as much backswing as you can manage. Remember to keep your eyes fixed on the ball.

Once again, finish off your kick with a strong follow through.

When you shoot at goal your volley must be controlled. For defense the volleying technique needs less control – sometimes it is a great advantage to send the ball soaring up field.

VOLLEY

INSIDE FOOT

The inside of the foot should be used for accurate passing. Its breadth helps you to control the ball and allows a greater margin for error. It is particularly useful for ground passing over short and medium ranges.

Using the inside of your foot to kick the ball is similar to the way a golfer uses a putter.

Place your non-kicking foot alongside the ball and adopt a square-on position with the knee of your kicking foot sticking outwards, almost at right-angles to the path of the ball.

Strike the ball firmly with the inside of your foot. It is a better to overhit than to underhit.

INSIDE FOOT

LEFT SWERVE

The low drive can be used to curve the ball as well as to kick it in a straight line. Curving the ball, also known as swerving the ball, involves striking the side of the ball rather than its centre point.

To swerve the ball to the left, strike the right-hand side of the ball with your instep. Make firm contact with the ball; it will not swerve if you just flick it.

LEFT SWERVE

RIGHT SWERVE

To swerve the ball to the right, strike the left-hand side of the ball with the outside of your right foot.

To perform this skill you need to approach the ball in a straighter line than usual and swing your leg across in front of your body.

Avoid the temptation to flick the ball; you will only achieve an effective swerve if you make a strong kicking movement.

RIGHT SWERVE

OVERHEAD KICK

Often known as a bicycle kick, the overhead kick can come to the rescue when you are faced with an attacking and awkwardly bouncing ball.

Thrust your hips and legs upwards so your body is in a

horizontal position, then hook the ball over your head. The higher you can raise your hips, the greater the power you can apply to your kick.

Keep your hands out to stop your fall.

OVERHEAD KICK

Heading skills

STANDING HEADER

Heading is an important soccer skill. It may seem painful to a novice, but once the correct technique is mastered it becomes as natural as kicking or catching.

The broad area of the forehead is flat and very strong and provides the perfect area for heading. With practice you will learn to direct your headed passes.

The golden rule is to move to meet the ball with your head, rather than let the ball strike you. If you attack the ball it will never hurt.

Position yourself either square-on to the approaching ball, or sideways with one foot in front of the other.

Use all your power to thrust your head at the ball; in particular, use your neck and leg muscles. It should seem as though you are throwing your head at the ball.

Remember that this technique will come to nothing if you close your eyes. Initially it might be tempting to do so, but the results will be more painful. Watch the ball all the way onto your forehead.

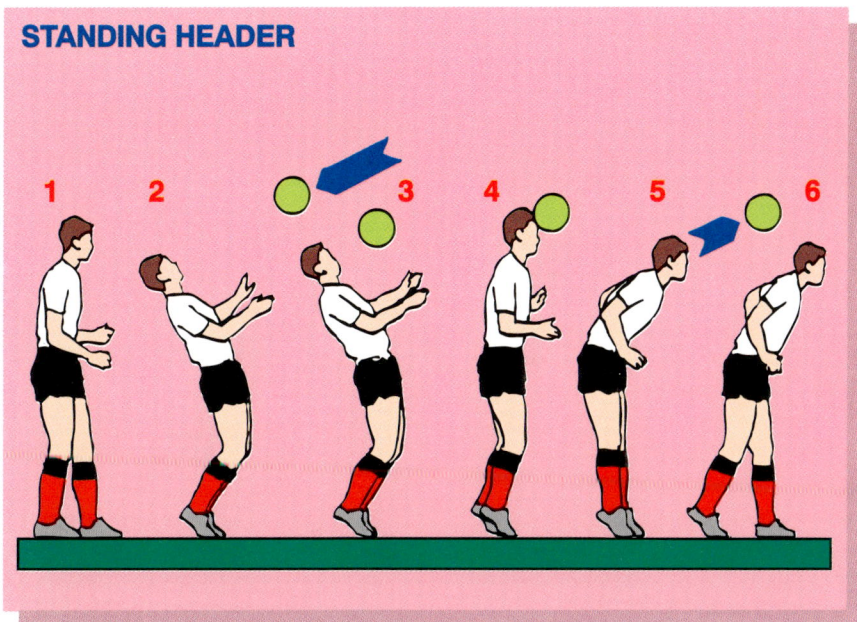

STANDING HEADER

JUMPING HEADER

Heading is most natural when you have to leap for the ball. Timing of the jump will come with practice. Just as you should not commit yourself too early, it can be fatal to be too late.

Take off from one foot when you jump for the ball. Practise so that you can take off from either foot.

Thrust your body upwards, using your arms and the upward swing of your other leg to gain momentum.

Once you are in the air, brace your body so that you can add power to your header. Keep your eyes fixed on the ball and do not be distracted by your surrounding team-mates and opponents.

JUMPING HEADER

With confidence you will be able to use other areas of the head to strike the ball. The back header, using the top of the forehead (not the back of the head), will enable you to guide the ball to players behind you.

SIDE HEADER

A very useful heading skill is the deflection of the ball from the side of your forehead to team-mates either side of you.

To perform a side header you barely need to move your head – simply allow the ball to glance off the side. You can increase the pace of the ball to reach team-mates further away by giving a firmer flick to the side.

SIDE HEADER

Control skills

INSIDE FOOT

Effective control of the ball can earn you the precious
seconds needed to avoid a challenge from an opponent or
to fire a shot at goal. The most basic method of control is
to stop the ball against the inside of your foot (the
broadest part of the foot). To cushion the impact of the
moving ball and stop it bouncing away, present the inside
of your foot to the ball, relax it as the ball arrives and pull
back at the point of contact. The ball will stop dead.

INSIDE FOOT

1   2   3   4

OUTSIDE FOOT

When you have developed your skills using the inside of
your foot, you can extend your control skills by using the
outside of your foot. Again the key to success is to

absorb the impact of the moving ball by withdrawing your controlling foot at the right moment. As the ball approaches, move your weight onto your standing leg and turn the outside of your controlling foot to meet the ball. Once you can stop the ball you should practise moving off with it in different directions. This will give variety to your control skills and make you better equipped to avoid tackles.

OUTSIDE FOOT

CHEST (1)

Soccer is played with the ball off the ground as well as on it, so you must develop techniques for controlling it in the air. Use your chest when the ball is dropping steeply and you have time to control it rather than head it away.

As with all types of control it is essential to get your body in line with the path of the ball. Take up a position with one leg in front of the other. Thrust out your chest and, as the ball drops, apply the cushioning technique (see page 24). The ball will conveniently fall at your feet. Take care not to use your arms and be penalized for handball.

CHEST (1)

CHEST (2)

If the ball is driven flat towards you at chest height, apply the technique described above but this time hunch your shoulders forward so that you are presenting a convex surface to the ball.

If the ball is bouncing up at you, control the ball with your chest and stomach. Line up with the path of the ball so that you can judge the bounce. Then lean over to meet it. Apply the cushioning technique (see page 24) and the ball will drop to the ground close to your feet.

You can add sophistication to all types of chest control by twisting your body; rather than simply killing the ball this will allow you to propel it in a new direction.

CHEST (2)

1   2   3   4

SOLE TRAP

SOLE TRAP

1   2   3   4

© DIAGRAM

Trapping the ball under the sole of your foot is a useful way to control a ball driven straight at you. Raise your foot to wedge the ball between the sole of your boot and the ground. Then pull your foot back slightly on impact to cushion the ball. The back spin this creates will bring the ball back towards you if it bounces away.

THIGH

If the ball is dropping below chest height, you can use your thigh to bring it down to your feet.

Like the chest, the thigh has a wide flat surface which is ideal for control. The golden rule is to position the flat surface (the front) of the thigh at right angles to the path of the ball. If the ball is dropping steeply, bend your knee and lift the controlling leg upwards. If the ball is driven horizontally towards you, bend your lower leg up behind you and drop your thigh so it is almost vertical. Again, apply the cushioning technique (see page 24).

THIGH

1   2   3   4

INSTEP

Using the instep or upper area of the foot to kill the ball is a refined skill. Developing it will improve your touch and control skills.

Imagine that you are trying to catch the ball on your instep. To cushion its impact, lift your controlling foot to meet the ball and, keeping your ankle relaxed, withdraw your foot as the ball arrives – the ball will follow the path of your foot to the ground.

As soon as the ball reaches the ground you can use it to the advantage of your team.

INSTEP

1 2 3 4

HEAD

Foot, thigh and chest are all vital areas of control, but your skills will only be complete if you learn to stop the ball with your head.

The key to this exercise is to position yourself in line with the ball when it is still high in the air. When the ball reaches your forehead, cushion its impact by gently moving your head back a little. With practice you will learn to guide the ball so you can move off in any direction you choose once it hits the ground.

HEAD

Dribbling and feinting skills

BODY FEINT LEFT

Dribbling is the soccer term for running with the ball. To run with the ball past opponents requires control and deception skills, known as feinting skills. Feinting involves using body movements to mislead your opponent.

The prerequisite for dribbling is control of the ball. It is very hard to dribble successfully if you cannot keep the ball within playing distance.

It is also important to be well balanced. You cannot expect to use feinting skills to unbalance your opponent if you are not balanced and fully in control yourself.

BODY FEINT LEFT

One way to unbalance your opponent is to pretend to move to one side of him and then to run past him on the other side. This move is called a body feint.

To body feint left, drop your left shoulder to suggest that you are going to move left (i.e. pass your opponent on his right side). Then quickly swerve to the right, passing your opponent on his left side. He will be caught off balance if your body feint has been successful.

Where possible try to dribble with the outside of the foot furthest away from the opponent. In the above example, use the outside of your right foot so your opponent has to stretch right across your body to get to the ball.

BODY FEINT RIGHT

The body feint right is similar to the body feint left, but this time you mislead your opponent into thinking you are moving right (by dropping your right shoulder). You then pass him by going left.

Try to cultivate the knack of looking away from the ball for a fraction of a second. Your opponent may follow your eyes and for a moment will be off guard.

Speed is vital. Once you have deceived your opponent you must move off quickly. Explosive pace is a tremendous asset in most soccer situations and especially in dribbling with the ball.

Be careful not to lose control of the ball by pushing it too far ahead. If there is space behind the opponent, you can push the ball there as long as you are sure you will be the first to reach it.

Another way to confuse a defender is by running at him with the ball without swerving.

Or, if you are in perfect control, you can tempt the defender into a rash challenge by 'showing' him the ball. This involves making him think that the ball is running

BODY FEINT RIGHT

1

2

3

4

away from you so that he commits himself to running for the ball. If you are in control you will reach the ball first and take it past him.

BALL FEINT

Another useful deception is to pretend to play the ball one way and then to lift your foot over the top of it and play it another way.

Try it with your right foot as though you are about to carry the ball to your left. The defender will assume that you are going to the left (his right). When he adjusts himself to counterattack, step over the ball and twist the other way. Then use the outside of your right foot to move the ball to the right.

Practise the skill with both feet and in both directions so if your opponent does not buy the first dummy you can throw him another in the opposite direction.

BALL FEINT

1   2   3   4

STOP FEINT

The skill of controlling the ball by stopping it with the sole of your foot can be used to outwit your opponent.

The objective in a stop feint is to pretend to stop and then to keep going, leaving your opponent behind.

Dribble the ball forward and then put your foot over the ball as if to stop it. When your opponent responds, accelerate past him for all you are worth.

STOP FEINT

Tackling skills

FRONT BLOCK TACKLE

Determination, balance and concentration are all factors
that will help you become a good tackler. The most basic
technique for robbing an opponent of the ball is the front
block tackle – a foot-to-foot confrontation.

When tackling it is always best to get as close as you can
to your opponent so you can use the weight of your
whole body to win the ball.

FRONT BLOCK TACKLE

Aim to make contact with the centre of the ball. If you hit it too high your foot will just slip over the top.

Keep your knee and ankle firm – as you would if you were making a strong pass with the inside of your foot. Adopt a compact position so that you can force the ball from your opponent.

SIDE BLOCK TACKLE

When the player you are challenging is moving in the same direction as you, use the side block tackle.

SIDE BLOCK TACKLE

Again position yourself as close as possible to your opponent, placing your non-tackling foot as near to the ball as you can.

Keep your tackling foot turned outwards so that you can make a full twist into the tackle. Then aim for the centre of the ball. Avoid touching your opponent, or make sure if you do that you touch the ball first. Bad tackling will concede free kicks and get you in trouble with the referee.

SLIDING TACKLE

Throughout a game of soccer, you are of maximum use to your side when you are on your feet; when you are on the ground you are virtually out of the game. However, in desperate circumstances you may need to throw yourself at the ball to recover it for your team.

The sliding tackle is an example. When an attacker is racing away with the ball and you cannot get close enough to make a block tackle, stretch your legs into a sliding position and try to knock the ball away.

This is a risky manoeuvre. If you miscalculate, you are almost certain to bring down your opponent, giving away a free kick or a penalty. If you miss entirely, you will leave him completely free. So pick your moment and then slide in.

Your tackling leg should be the one furthest from your opponent. Try to knock the ball a long way; if it simply falls to another attacker you will be in no position to make another challenge.

SLIDING TACKLE

SLIDING BLOCK TACKLE

One way to recover from a sliding tackle is to win the ball for yourself rather than just knocking it away. This can be achieved if you make a block challenge at the end of your slide.

The technique is the same as for the sliding tackle except

that you attack the ball in a front block position (see pages 36 and 37).

Your impetus will tend to carry you across the path of the ball rather than to it, so it is very important to quickly recover your balance if you are to compete for possession.

SLIDING BLOCK TACKLE

The risk is that you lose the confrontation and your opponent takes the ball on, leaving you on the ground in his wake. The more conventional sliding tackle has a higher rate of success, but of course will not win the ball for you.

Goalkeeping skills

CATCHING

As goalkeeper, you have the advantage of being allowed to use your hands – and you must use them; keep your feet and the rest of your body for emergencies only. Always catch the ball with both hands and pull it into your body (1); you can then be sure that it will not wriggle free. When the ball is below chest height, point your fingers downwards, curl up your arms as it arrives and then clutch it to your chest. When it is above chest height, point your fingers upwards with thumbs touching so that your hands make a basket for the ball to drop in (2). The most embarrassing moment for a goalkeeper is

CATCHING

when the ball slips through his legs over the line, so in fielding the ball always remember to keep your legs together. As with all goalkeeping techniques, position yourself in line with the approaching ball. Bend from the waist and slightly at the knees and pick the ball up with both hands (**3**). For extra safety, go down on one knee so that the ball has no chance of passing the barrier of your thigh (**4**).

CATCHING

PUNCHING AND PUSHING

Catching is the primary goalkeeping skill; only when this presents a risk should the ball be pushed away or punched. For instance, it is sometimes better to punch the ball away if it is wet and slippery or when opposing forwards are bearing down on you. To punch the ball, watch it all the way as it approaches (**1**). Use both hands to strike the ball hard (**2**); do not just pat it. The further away from the goal it goes the safer it is.

PUNCHING AND PUSHING

Sometimes neither a catch nor a punch are possible. In these circumstances, you must push the ball to safety. It is best to use both hands to push the ball away – and the safest place is behind your goal. Do not just pat the ball out of the goal mouth.

DIVING

Your dive to save is a test of technique as well as reflexes. The skill involves a sideways dive, with your body facing the ball and not the ground (**1**, see over).

In this sideways position you can watch the ball right into your hands. The skill also involves making a clean mid-air catch. Once in your hands, pull the ball close to your body before you land to avoid losing it when you hit the turf.

Low shots are the hardest to dive for (**2**). Aim to get low as quickly as possible and remember to position yourself sideways so you can watch the ball and stop it running underneath your body.

When diving at an opponent's feet, you are less likely to be hurt if you act positively. Dive at the ball as the opponent prepares to shoot. Remember to keep a sideways position. Pulling the ball into your chest will help you retain possession as well as protect you from your opponent's kick.

DIVING

1

DIVING

2

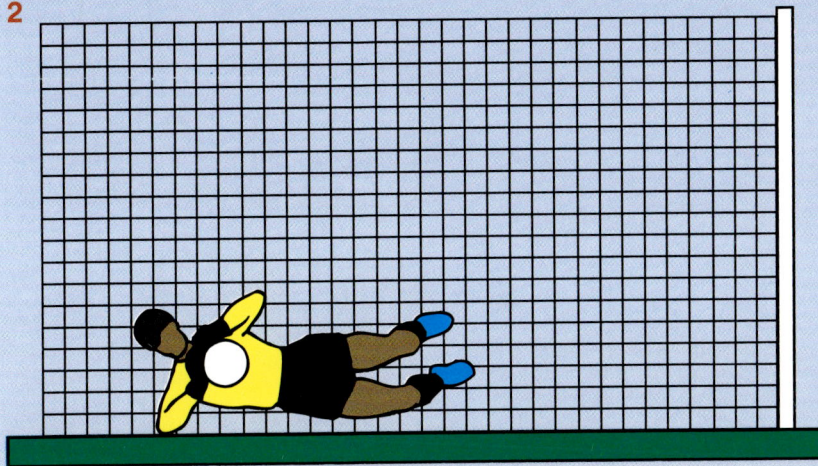

DISTRIBUTING THE BALL

When you have made your save and gained possession you must use the ball to the benefit of your team. Concentrate on achieving length and accuracy in your kick. When you volley from your hands make sure that you line up with the ball and kick in a straight line; do not kick across the path of the ball. Swing your leg as fast as possible, following through after contact (**1**, *see over*).

Alternatively, you can throw the ball – one-handed overarm or underarm (**2**, *see over*). Again the key is accuracy. Only throw the ball close to your own goal if it is completely safe to do so.

DISTRIBUTING THE BALL

1

2

Remember that under the rules you are only allowed to take a total of four paces in possession of the ball before releasing it, and that you may not roll or dribble the ball once you have handled it.